*Everyone's life is a journey
and sometimes
the roads that we travel
are more mysterious and magical
than we ever imagined.*

Dedication

To the One Who Changed My Life

In a world full of changes
where the change of seasons
dances with the changing times
there is one thing
that will never
CHANGE...

I LOVE YOU

Is It Time to Make a

CHANGE?

Positive Thoughts for When
Life Presents You with a New Direction

Deanna Beisser

Blue Mountain Press ™

SPS Studios, Inc., Boulder, Colorado

Library of Congress Catalog Card Number: 99-16856
ISBN: 0-88396-528-3

Certain trademarks are used under license.

The following works have previously appeared in Blue Mountain Arts® publications: "Anything Is Possible," "Special People," "Let Your Life Be a Wonderful Adventure," "Promise Yourself Only the Best," "Be Who You Are," "When You're True to Yourself, Life Is Everything You Want It to Be," and "Keep Believing in Yourself."

Manufactured in China
Second Printing in Hardcover: October 2001

♻ This book is printed on recycled paper.

This book is printed on fine quality, laid embossed, 80 lb. paper. This paper has been specially produced to be acid free (neutral pH) and contains no groundwood or unbleached pulp. It conforms with all the requirements of the American National Standards Institute, Inc., so as to ensure that this book will last and be enjoyed by future generations.

Library of Congress Cataloging-in-Publication Data

. Beisser, Deanna.
   Is it time to make a change? / Deanna Beisser.
      p.   cm.
   ISBN 0-88396-528-3 (alk. paper)
   1. Life change events Poetry. 2. Conduct of life Poetry. I. Title.
PS3552.E43518   1999
811'.54–dc21   99-16856
                                                                      CIP

SPS Studios, Inc.
P.O. Box 4549, Boulder, Colorado 80306

Introduction

Life is a continuous collection of changes. Sadly or strangely, whichever way you choose to think of it, as people grow older, they generally tend to reduce their likelihood of experiencing change and challenges. Upon reaching a stage in life when we are intellectually superior to our days of youth, most of us tend to disregard the wondrous opportunities we are given to explore life's endless mysteries. Security and familiarity seem to bring comfort and satisfaction. The irony is that it is in our older years that we are best equipped to deal with change and enjoy the vast array of experiences that it produces.

Life is the ongoing accumulation of each and every person who has ever lived. It is the interactions of all things at any given moment. All living organisms have a relationship and a significance toward one another... we exist in this world together, each of us with our own particular gift to bestow. The importance of understanding that every one of us has something of value to share in this life is what changes one day to the next.

I have enjoyed writing each and every verse included in this book, some of which are my own heartfelt emotions and many of which are those of the ones I love. I hope you will enjoy them as well.

When the songs of your heart
start singing,
you should gratefully listen...
for the harmony is
that which will bring you
happiness
and the melody is
the voice of your true spirit.

Anything Is Possible

Life holds no promises
as to what will come your way.
You must search for your own ideals
and work toward reaching them.
Life makes no guarantees
as to what you'll have.
It just gives you time to make choices
and to take chances
and to discover whatever secrets
might come your way.
If you are willing to take
the opportunities you are given
and utilize the abilities you have,
you will constantly fill your life
with special moments
and unforgettable times.

No one knows the mysteries of life
or its ultimate meaning,
but for those who are willing
to believe in their dreams
and in themselves,
life is a precious gift
in which anything is possible.

It's Never Too Late
to Make a Change

At any time, you can decide to
change the road you're on in life, take
a new direction, follow a new trail. You
are the only one who really knows what
you want from life and if you're on the
right road for you. You are the only one
who can fulfill your dreams and receive
the joys and happiness that come from
reaching those aspirations and goals.

Don't expect others to be responsible
for your happiness and your success. You
must take control and be in charge of
your destiny and day-to-day situations.
Take advice (most of the time it's free!)
and listen to what others have to say and
what concerns they have; it's important
to have different points of view. But
always validate those words of wisdom
with your own set of standards and
make sure that the advice has meaning to
your sense of reality.

You must understand yourself enough to know what you want in life and what desires you believe are worthwhile for your future. You need to depend upon yourself and your talents. Appreciate others for their personal skills and abilities, but always continue to focus on your own strengths and energies. Life is much too short to spend it worrying about someone else's accomplishments or expecting someone else to be responsible for making your life better.

If you have dreams, then you have a purpose. You have something to believe in and work toward obtaining. Dedicate yourself to yourself. Promise yourself a life filled with love, and then whatever roads you travel will be the roads you want them to be.

Special People

Special people are those
who have the ability to share
   their lives with others.
They are honest in word and deed,
they are sincere and compassionate,
and they always make sure that
   love is a part of everything.
Special people are those who have the ability
to give to others
and help them with the changes
   that come their way.
They are not afraid
of being vulnerable;
they believe in their uniqueness
   and are proud to be who they are.
Special people are those who
allow themselves the pleasures
of being close to others
   and caring about their happiness.
They have come to understand
that love is what makes
the difference in life.
Special people are those who
truly make life beautiful.

Be a Dreamer

Be someone who inspires
the people around you
by the way you live your life
and the way you treat others.
Stay focused on your future
and be willing to give all that you are
to make your dreams come true.
Encourage others,
and support them
with your strong beliefs.
Be a motivated person
who takes chances when
they present themselves.
Don't wait or worry about tomorrow;
just keep focused on
what's happening today.
Be someone
who looks forward
to challenges
and fully accepts
both the joys and struggles
that come to someone who dreams.

Life Is a Lesson We Learn Day After Day

I have learned so many lessons in my life.
I have discovered how to enjoy
the people and places that surround me,
to appreciate the here and now.
I have grown and changed through
expressing my thoughts and feelings
to family and friends.
I have given of myself to them when times
were good and when they were not,
and the bond of understanding that we
feel for one another has taken
our hearts and woven them together.

Life is a series of transitions
and a collection of interactions with others.
It is a journey through time that
gathers together so many emotions
and allows us all to cherish
the truths that we believe in
and to respect others for theirs.

Life proceeds forward,
and it happens over and over again
as each day begins and ends.
It holds millions of mysteries for each of us
to explore and incorporate into our lives.
We are each the center of our own life
and by focusing on ourselves
and understanding our desires and dreams,
we can fulfill our true spirits and find
a sense of happiness in all that we do.

I create the roads that I will follow.
My life is an ongoing experience
that fascinates and enlightens me.
I am forever questioning
my thoughts and feelings
and the never-ending illusive truths that
keep me pondering the mysteries of life.
I have no words of wisdom to explain
what life should or should not be,
but I do know this:

> "Every breath is counted
> and time is timeless.
> One day I will be gone."

Take Time to Think About
What Truly Makes You Happy

It's all right to be fearful
of the unknown;
it's smart to walk slowly
into the darkness.
It's all right to think twice
about making changes;
it's wise to look ahead in all directions
before starting out on a new road.
It's all right to reconsider
and reevaluate some of your feelings;
it's good to let your emotions settle down
before you rearrange your life
and your dreams.
Difficult times require
difficult decisions to be made,
and the easy answers
that once solved your problems
are no longer the right answers.

Take some time to really think about
what you want to do
with your life and future.
Be honest with yourself.
Ask yourself if you are happy
the way you are living now
or if you need to make a change.
Happiness comes to those
who are willing to believe in it
and who create it within their own lives.
You deserve to be happy.
You deserve to be treated with respect.
Your life should be filled with good times,
not troubled ones.
Take some time and think about yourself.

Lifeline

Each of us is born on a line;
from the moment of conception
to the moment of our death,
we are all on a lifeline.
The passage from one point to the next
is filled with experiences and interactions,
and each of us will express our true spirit
as these moments present themselves.
The journey is one of progression;
it is a contemplation of the future.
We are all searching for something,
traveling toward our dreams.
What exists now is really all that ever exists;
we cannot feel the past of a thousand years
nor can we touch the lifeline of tomorrow.
We dance to the music of here and now;
we sing the songs of today.
We have an understanding about who we are
and what destiny is ours to fulfill.

Let the winds of change blow all around you
and follow your lifeline wherever it may lead,
knowing that others are pursuing their fate
on different pathways leading them
in different directions.
Each and every one of us
will find a true sense of purpose
if we travel our own roads
on our own lifeline.

Let Your Life Be a Wonderful Adventure!

Let your life be an exploration.
Let people and places be
    a part of your life,
and experience each and every
    unique situation
with a sense of wonder and delight.

Look in all directions to seek out
the answers you long to know,
and discover the secrets that
keep questioning your heart.
Be willing to make changes and
be ready to face the challenges.
Accept the opportunities
    that present themselves,
and endure and cope with
    the difficulties
that can arise from time to time.

Remember that there is no one way
    to live your life,
but a thousand different ways for
    each of us to be.
Make your life the way
    you want it to be
and create a lifestyle that
    brings you happiness.
Search for your true meaning in life
by devoting yourself to your ideals,
and enjoy your wonderful adventure
    through time
by making every day special.

Allow Your Own Inner Light
to Guide You

There comes a time when you
    must stand alone.
You must feel confident enough
    within yourself
to follow your own dreams.
You must be willing
    to make sacrifices.
You must be capable of
    changing and rearranging
    your priorities
so that your final goal
    can be achieved.
Sometimes, familiarity and comfort
    need to be challenged.
There are times when you must
    take a few extra chances
and create your own realities.
Be strong enough to at least try
    to make your life better.
Be confident enough that
    you won't settle for a compromise
just to get by.
Appreciate yourself by allowing yourself
    the opportunities to grow, develop,
and find your true sense of purpose
    in this life.
Don't stand in someone else's shadow
    when it's your sunlight
that should lead the way.

Embracing Change

I find it a bit amusing
when people talk about CHANGE...
how they delicately
and ever so gently whisper its name.
Some are intimidated by or insecure about
its presence,
while others are politely respectful
of its immense power.

CHANGE...
With a smile or a tear,
it touches our lives day in and day out,
the relentless, inevitable warrior of fate.
It can arrive at any moment in life,
but we must not feel threatened by it
or fearful.
Instead, when change is upon us,
we should open our eyes wider
with amazement and enthusiasm;
we should extend our arms further,
and embrace the world around us.

CHANGE...
Let it jolt you, push and pull you.
Let it challenge you.
Know in your heart that change
is what gives you the chance
to be yourself
and the opportunity to make your life
everything you want it to be.

Wake-Up Call

Yesterday I stood looking at my face
in the mirror,
staring at myself in actual amazement.
I looked older,
my hair looked tired,
and the sparkle that once shined
in my eyes as a child had faded.
There was a seriousness
that had taken its place.
At that moment,
a sense of urgency and determination
was awakened in me.
That face in the mirror
was changing right in front of me.
I could have told myself
it was just a bad hair day,
but deep inside I knew that
this was a transition I needed to face,
literally... face to face.
I smiled at myself with one of those
you-don't-look-so-bad kind of smiles,
but that didn't work.
So I tried to make my smile bigger and brighter,
hoping to find a renewed spirit somewhere,
but that didn't help either.
This was my wake-up call –
time to start doing the things I want to do,
time to think about making some changes,
time to get my life going.
And it wouldn't hurt to run a comb
through my hair, too!

As you awaken to the changes
that are surrounding your life,
you must also stop
and reminisce about your past.
Who you are is an accumulation of
everything that you once were,
the total sum of each and every thought
you have ever had
and every single feeling
you have ever known.
Change is what keeps us
constantly striving to be more
than we were before.
Life shines brightly for those who
experience the changes they are given.
Life is the interaction of all things,
and we must learn to respect everyone,
as we all will journey in different directions.
To accept life as a passage through time
is to understand that people will indeed
fulfill their own destinies
as they travel the roads
only they alone can travel.
Let your life be an adventure...
look for the invisible,
listen to the silences,
touch your imagination,
and make each day something special.
You are your life,
and by believing in change,
you are believing in yourself
and everything that you will be.

It's Up to You!

It may be easier to give up
than it is to keep going
It may be easier to say
it's someone else's fault
than to take the blame yourself
It may be easier to make excuses
than to offer apologies

but there's no guarantee that
the easy way through life
is the best way
Make your travels through time worthwhile
Choose the roads that allow you
opportunities to grow and change
Look for adventures that challenge
your abilities
and find mysteries in life
that excite your sense of wonder
Search for the truths that you believe in
and discover as many secrets about life
as you can
It is up to you to create your life
Your unique spirit needs to explore the world
and be an active part of every day
Don't be so concerned about finding
the easiest roads to travel
but follow the roads that lead you toward
being the person you really want to be
Remember, the important things in life
are the things that <u>you</u> believe are important

There is
a free spirit and a true spirit
within each of us.
Our free spirit wants to kiss the wind
whenever it gently touches our life.
It wants to sail away to some
enchanted paradise.
Our true spirit wants to embrace
the moon and stars
and cherish their magic.
It is the combination of both
our free spirit and our true spirit
that enables us to discover
the mysteries of our soul.

Your Happiness Depends
on One Person...
You!

Every day, tell yourself
to be ready for change.
Be ready for challenges that may come
or opportunities that may present themselves.

Every day, prepare yourself to make choices
about what you want from life
and what you plan on in the future.
Remind yourself to follow through
on your ideas and to continually work
toward their success.

Every day, remind yourself
to think positively about things,
to take whatever happens
and find something good in it, to be hopeful.
Every day when you get up, realize
that no matter what problems you have
or what worries there are in your life,
you are in control of your destiny
and you can make a difference
in anything you choose to do.
Your happiness doesn't depend
on someone else; it depends on you
and whether you're willing to accept
the situations you've been given.
Do not get up each morning
dreading what you have to do,
but look forward to the unbelievably
unique lifestyle that you possess.
You may have stress and some complications
here and there to deal with,
but smile to yourself knowing
that you're in charge,
that you can handle your life,
and that you're going to make it the best you can.

Promise Yourself
Only the Best

Promise yourself
to dream more and hesitate less.
To believe in yourself more
and judge yourself less by
the accomplishments of others.
To appreciate your family
and friends
for all the wonderful ways
they make your life better.
Promise yourself
to accept life as it comes
and truly make each day special.
To become more independent
and more willing to change.
To fill your life
with special times,
and make your dreams come true.

Time Is on Your Side

You cannot turn back the hands of time.
Time moves forward whether you want it to or not.
It allows us opportunities to constantly change.
The only inhibitory factor lies within ourselves.
We are the ones holding ourselves back;
we are the ones trying to out-guess life;
we are the ones who say: "I can't" or "Not now"
or "It's just not meant to be"...
But the truth of the matter is this...
Time says, "YES"; it says, "Do it now"
because "anything is possible."
Time truly believes in "JUST TRY."
It's funny how we talk ourselves out of
so many wonderful chances to be
all that we want to be.
It seems that only a few true adventurers
listen to what "TIME" has to say...
and they are the ones enjoying themselves
because they know
time is on their side.

Competition Is an Opportunity
for Us to Give Our Best

Competition is important;
it is a part of life
that makes us all
try our best and give our best.
Competition is the opportunity
to reach a little further
and aim a little higher.

Competition is the excitement
that rises within us
to excel and to challenge ourselves.
It doesn't always mean
winning or losing,
but rather participating
in activities that require
dedication and determination.
Not everyone can be first,
but everyone can strive for
their own personal goals.

In life, each of us
accomplishes our own dreams
and contributes to others
by being a part of the whole.
Competition is a wonderful chance
to experience the beauty
of being ourselves
and seeing how special we really are.

A Way of Life

If you give your life
hopes and dreams,
you will find them
when you need them...

If you believe in yourself
and the abilities you possess,
you will accomplish your goals
and feel proud of who you are...

If you enjoy each and every day
and appreciate all that it has to offer,
you will be rewarded time and time again
with unexpected pleasures.

It is the way you look at your life
that makes all the difference...
Your life is a matter of perception;
you can search for sunshine behind clouds
or look for rain hiding in blue skies.

Words to Remember Every Day

Be patient today with others;
they need someone who will
take the time to listen...

Be giving today with others;
they need someone who will share...

Be honest today with others;
they need someone whom they can trust...

Be sincere today with others;
they need someone who really cares...

Be understanding today with others;
they need someone who is not judgmental...

Be happy today with others;
they need someone who will smile...

Life challenges us all each and every day;
that is why
it is so very important to remember...

Be gentle today with others;
they need someone to be a friend.

Not Every Dream Comes True, but the Pursuit Can Still Lead Us to Happiness

The reason why
some dreams don't come true
isn't because you didn't give enough
or that you didn't work hard enough
or allow yourself the time you needed.
Certain dreams in our lives
are just not meant to come true.
But those dreams are a part of our lives
that exist as guiding lights
and direction signs to keep us headed
on the right path.

We follow certain dreams
to a particular point in time,
and then it's necessary
to believe in new dreams
and search out new horizons.
Our lives are constantly changing,
making it possible for all of us
to constantly change, too,
providing us with opportunities
to experience as much of life
as we so desire.
The completeness of our lives
doesn't depend on all our dreams
coming true,
but rather the happiness we experience
in following the different dreams
we hold in our hearts.
Every day holds a new dream,
and every day there's a chance
of dreams coming true.

It's Important to Always Keep Changing

There once was a time
when I thought I could
change the world.
Now I realize that
all I need to do
is work on changing myself.
I can make things better.

There have been times in my life
when my hopes and dreams
were based on others.
Now I realize that
all I really need is
to have faith in who I am.
I can believe in myself and find happiness.

And there are times in my life
when it would be easier to give up or give in.
But then I realize that
all I need to do is
keep trying,
keep believing,
and always keep changing,
because that is what life is all about...
CHANGE!

Today!

When does the child vanish
and the adult appear?
When do we cross the line in time
that takes away the toys
and fills our hands with tools?
When do we know
which road to travel
and which paths only turn into circles?
When do we trust our feelings
and share our love with one another?
When do we take the chance
to say we care?

It's not too late
to slow down a bit
and take some time for ourselves.
Even when we're fully grown,
there is still a little bit
of the child within us.
When is it time to begin
to truly enjoy life?
Today!

It's Okay to Be Lonely...
for a little while

It's okay to be lonely
and not have to pretend
that everything is fine,
that you're always on time,
that poems all must rhyme.

It's okay to be lonely,
and you don't have to hide your tears
or carry a smile around for years
or deny or cover up your fears.

It's okay to be lonely,
to say you've had a bad day,
that you just want to get away,
and maybe, just maybe,
you want to be lonely... for a little while.

All Things Come in Time...

It is a wise man who allows his time to come to him
as he is working toward his dreams.
Getting up each morning,
we all have opportunities
to direct some aspects of our lives.
When we promote ourselves in a positive way
and keep our attitudes toward changes hopeful,
we enable ourselves to reach
whatever dreams we are pursuing.
Life has a fascinating way
of entertaining us the best
when we are entertaining ourselves
with our hearts' desires.
Our day-to-day experiences are truly ours alone,
so concentrate on the things that make you
feel good about yourself
and don't worry about time,
because one of these days...
it will be your time to shine!

Find time in life
for quiet moments
because they will balance out times of turmoil...
Difficult times will not last forever.

Make time in life
for love and sharing,
to let others know that you care...
Enjoy today by being here and now.

Always keep time for yourself,
and never lose sight of your hopes and dreams.
Your life is up to you,
so take time to believe
knowing that even on cloudy nights,
the stars are still shining.

Nature Is Our Best Teacher

Nature exists just as it is,
intimidated by no one.
In the world of nature,
what is known as spirit is that which is.
Creatures do not alter their existence
to be other than they are;
their spirits remain true.

In nature,
the passage of time,
like the change of seasons,
is endless and forever.
Time is not measured; it just exists.
As people, we try to measure everything;
we want to calculate or evaluate time,
and most definitely, we want to control it.

We could learn many things from nature.
One very important truth
would be simply to be yourself...
for that is your true spirit.
Another valuable lesson is
to live for today,
to be a part of the changes
and processes of now,
for it is in experiencing this moment
that you will be ready to experience the next.
If you live your life touching the present,
you will always be living your life
completely.

We fool ourselves sometimes into
thinking that life is more complicated
or confusing or mysterious than it really is.
Life is made up of fundamental truths.
It is the simplicity that baffles us;
we tend to defy the universal significance
of the natural laws that exist.
Life is a personal journey to which
each of us must draw our own conclusions
and discover our own realities.
It is a rather elementary adventure,
but we must all see the world for ourselves
and accept life for what it is,
for only then can we understand its secrets.
Life really isn't as complicated or confusing
as everyone makes it out to be...

The mystery is really no mystery,
other than people making it so.

Don't fear your last day
Any day could be final
Live your life today

Be Who You Are

Let the true spirit of who you are
shine through in all that you do.
Let your hopes and dreams
always guide you in the direction
that you definitely believe in.
Let the love that is within your heart
never stop being the most important
and beautiful part of your life.
Travel through time not as one alone,
but as one among the many;
reach out to those who need your
gentle spirit and caring ways.
Make your passage through time
an endless journey of love.

I will not pretend
to be anyone but me –
I am as I am

Breaking Old Habits

Some habits are more difficult
to change than others.
Some trains of thought seem
to always run along the same lines
and follow the same tracks,
occasionally becoming derailed
by enlightenment.
I know that for myself,
I tend to control my life
and focus my energies within
the boundaries I have rendered acceptable,
precluding many alternatives.
I adapt to change as I must,
and I do it willingly in most cases,
but I do notice that I'm not as open
as I should be to life's variations.
I feel comfortable with my routines
and obligations,
yet my inner spirit sends me messages
from time to time, saying...
Discovery is our entertainment in life,
experimentation is our participation in life,
and passage from one moment to the next
is life's way of telling us that
life is timeless...
we are not.

Life comes in waves...
a splash of excitement
moves you toward
a dream you've dreamed for a lifetime.
Another push or pull from any direction
guides you even closer
to the places you long to explore.
Life carries you along
with a gentle flow of changes and challenges,
and you float into tomorrow
knowing that another wave will be there for you
and you will be waiting to go.

A Motto for Living
Life to Its Fullest

Refuse to be unhappy;
   be cheerful instead.
Refuse to let your troubles multiply;
   just take them one by one.
Organize your time; keep your life simple
   and exactly the way you want it.
Refuse to complain about things;
   learn to improve your surroundings
and create your world
   the way you believe it should be.
Refuse to dwell on the mistakes
   or disappointments
that are sometimes a part of life;
instead learn how you can
   make things better.
Be optimistic.
Be energetic and positive
   about the things you do,
and always hope for the best.
Believe in yourself at all times
   and in all aspects of your life.
Before you know it,
those wonderful dreams
you have believed in all your life
   will come true,
and your life will be
the happy and successful life
   that it was meant to be.

Isn't It Time to
Feel Good About Yourself?

So many people try to hide their pain,
pretending that if they don't talk about
their worries and fears
then they don't really exist.
There are people who smile on the outside,
making light and carefree conversations
to prevent their intimate emotions
from being exposed.
Their personal doubts and insecurities
travel uninvited across their minds,
haunting them in the night.
It is a terrible burden to bear
to always question yourself
and feel as if no one understands you.
Let your self-doubts vanish into the shadows;
show your true spirit to everyone you meet.
All people must travel through life
not as one alone, but as a caravan of people
who will each experience their own set
of circumstances.
Your life is everything that encircles you,
and it's important
not to judge yourself critically
but to understand yourself,
not to restrict your emotions
but to express them,
not to limit yourself
but to search out every new horizon.
There are too many people
trying to be somebody else.
Isn't it time to be who you are,
and isn't it time
to feel good about yourself?

We Each Have
the Power to Choose

The wind changes directions
a hundred times or more a day.
It has no goal or focus to be
anything more than itself.
The wind is free to come and go
as it pleases.
But people, on the other hand,
have an inner desire to accomplish,
to achieve, to be productive.
It is a human quality that enables people
to select which way they want to go
and to determine how fast or how slow
their journey will be.
People have the power to choose
the roads they will travel.
They must never forget that
they are in control of their lives.

So let the wind blow in your face
and circle around you
as you live day to day,
but know in your heart
that you are the one,
the only one,
who really knows which way
the wind blows
for you.

When You're True to Yourself, Life Is Everything You Want It to Be

One of the most valuable lessons
you can ever learn in life is that
all your dreams may not come true.
You reach a point in your life
when you realize that what you want
isn't always what you need.
You come to understand yourself
for the real feelings
you hold inside your heart,
and not the feelings
that others want you to have.

When you begin to learn
what life means to you
and how you are going to spend
your time and energy,
you realize that life is
only what you believe it to be.
If you want happiness,
then it is up to you to make yourself happy,
and not wait for someone else to do it.

In the end, no one else can make you happy;
happiness comes from within.
It is enjoying life for yourself
and appreciating others
as they join you in the things you do.
You may learn a lot of
different lessons in your life,
but the most important of all
is realizing that life is
everything you want it to be;
you just have to believe in yourself,
believe in others,
and enjoy the changes of life
as they come your way.

From time to time,
we all feel a little disappointed
with our lives and perhaps the people in them.
We start questioning our daily routines;
a sense of loneliness touches our hearts,
and we wonder what life is really all about.
When you reach this point in your life,
take a moment and forget about
what has gone before...
and start believing in
what you really want today.
It is by redirecting our lives that we can keep
ourselves headed in the right direction,
and it is by standing still that
we allow time to just pass us by.
It is looking at a sunrise or a sunset
and appreciating its beauty for ourselves
that enables us to understand
some of life's mysteries.
No two people see the world the same way,
nor do they think or feel
or even experience things around them
with the same exact perception.
Don't try to mold yourself or your life
into a design that isn't you;
rather, paint your days
with all the colors you so desire
and enjoy the artwork that you alone
can create.

Every day
I look around me
and see people
who have problems
far greater than mine
Yet they confront life
with a courageous and honest
determination within themselves
It makes me stop and realize
how small my worries are in comparison
and how I should try that much harder
to be happy, tolerant
understanding, and caring
toward others
It encourages me to believe
in my own abilities
but most of all
to be thankful for all I have
every day of my life.

In my life,
I will not try to predict events
before they have happened
or cast final judgments on situations
that are ongoing in my life.
I have learned that
at any given moment
a smile can change one's direction,
and who is to know
when a smile will come your way.

I have discovered lately
the difference
between those individuals
who are successful
and those who are waiting for success.
People who are successful
have found a way to incorporate themselves
and their dreams into a working reality.
They are continually infusing their dreams
into each and every minute of the day.
They are changing and striving,
preparing and providing.
They are not waiting for a chance...
but are taking the chance.
They are not hesitating
but participating.
They are dedicated, hard workers.
Success grows from sacrifice and commitment.
Those who wait for their dreams to materialize
will continue to do just that,
while others are working and changing
to make their dreams come true.

---

*If you continue to climb mountains
you will be able to stand
above the hills,
and you will see the horizon
in all directions.*

Great Achievers

I am fascinated by other people's
creativity and productivity.
I am in awe of their dedication
and determination to fulfill
their talents and desires.
Great achievers are those who
follow the yearnings of their souls.
They are those who challenge themselves
with daily sacrifices
and relentlessly endure the
inconveniences and consequences
that occur as a result of their goals.
They are focused on developing themselves,
mastering their unique abilities,
and making their dreams a part
of their lifestyles.
They create their own lives
by never wasting a single day
and possessing the inner strength
to carry on through all of life's changes
with an open mind
and a hopeful heart.

There is no reason to waste today.
You are traveling through time
into the future.
Tomorrow is beyond here and now.

I have known many different kinds
of people in my life...
I've met men who are sensitive and caring
and men who are cruel and calculating.
I've known women who are sincere and honest
and women who are jealous and hateful.
I've seen smiles filled with lies
and tears wet with truths.
I've shared time with those who have needed me,
and I've been by myself when I was in need.
I've been associated with people
who are dreamers but not doers
and with people who make promises
but never keep them.
I've found myself learning how to
understand all these personalities
and to avoid those that
cause my life sadness.

My soul yearns for those who
still believe in life's truths
of honesty
of sincerity
of compassion
and of true friendship.
But most of all,
I long to know those few people who
really know what love is
and how to be a loving person.
I long for a place where people can
get together and talk to one another
about the things that matter,
like being friends and caring about
the dreams that we all believe in.
I long for a time when
friendship and love are important
and the best parts of our lives.

You Must Let It Go

You cannot erase the past;
you must let it go.
You cannot change yesterday;
you must accept the lessons learned.
You cannot stop time
or stand still in a world
racing around in circles;
you must dance with the wind
and sing with the songs
that are playing.
Let whatever mistakes you have made
remain in the shadows
of times gone by,
and let love be the answer
to the mysteries in life.

Keep looking...
for the peacefulness
you are searching for
Keep believing...
in the contentment
you talk so endlessly about
Keep trying...
to be all that you are.

Remember...
the magic in life ends
whenever you decide
you have everything.

The Gift of Time

Wake up every morning
and feel thankful for a new day!
Don't waste it by
backtracking too far into yesterday
or reaching too far into tomorrow.
Time is a gift that we all sometimes
let slip away —
we forget how important it is
to enjoy our lives
and to help others enjoy theirs.
If you need to make changes in your life,
make them;
create a lifestyle
that makes you feel complete.
Life is all around you;
the gift of time allows you
endless possibilities.
Keep moving forward,
and try to make every day
your best day.

Let Your Spirit Guide You

There is no place you can go to hide
from the thoughts that you keep contemplating
over and over inside your mind.
There is no place you can venture
where your true emotions will be concealed
and the secrets of your heart will not show.
There is no place in this whole wide world
you can travel to where your spirit
does not direct or guide you
toward your destiny.

Life is the experience of being YOU;
no one can ever be someone other
than who they are.
The beauty found in each and every person
is the essence of life.
Simply... you are who you are
and for whatever time you have to be,
you must not try to shadow yourself,
but, rather, express yourself.

Is It Time to Make a Change?

Do you accept yourself
for everything that you are?
Do you look at yourself
openly and honestly
and appreciate the person you call "me"?
There's no need for a mirror
to see your reflection
because your face changes from day to day;
it is what is inside your heart
that tells the true story of your life.
You need to be totally truthful
about who you really are.
Are you someone who feels secure
with yourself,
or are you looking for someone else
to make you feel content?
Are you someone who reaches out
to give to others
or are you looking for protection?
Are you someone who smiles naturally
or do you hide behind social politeness?
Are you someone who finds fault
in the world around you
or are you willing to listen to solutions?
Are you the kind of person
you really want to be
or is it time to make a change?

Feel the Power Within You

Listen to the words of wisdom
whispering within your mind —
they want to lead you
in the right directions.
Quietly adhere to your inner voice
that speaks to you through your emotions;
allow your heart the freedom
to make you happy.
Be truthful to yourself,
and be willing to share your uniqueness
in whatever creative fashion
your talents provide.
This is life at its best.
In fact, this is life exactly as it is...
it is today — here and now.
So if you feel the power
to move and change,
then let your life flow
knowing that it is time to go.
But if you need some more time
to think about your hopes and dreams,
then find a sense of peace in staying.

Before I leave this world,
I want to tell my children
a few very important things
about who I am
and what I believe.
It may not make a difference
in the big scheme of things,
but at least for me,
I will feel as if
I shared my heart
and the truths of my soul.
I want them to know that my spirit
danced with each new day
and quietly kissed each evening good-night,
that I loved them with all that I am,
and that wherever their journeys lead them,
my love will be there, too.

You Can Be Anything
You Dream Of

Every day has
its own rewards
and its own unique challenges.
None of us has
the same exact worries
or responsibilities,
because life is shaped
around each of us
as individuals.
It's important to remember that
we all create our own worlds.
Who we are and the way we act
are how we control our lives.
There are endless opportunities
for us to change and rearrange
the day-to-day moments
we are given.
It's up to each of us to decide
which way we want to go;
how far or how fast
we go in life are the choices
we all must make for ourselves.

Allow Each Day to Sing Its Own Unique Song for You

Every day, there is a different
　　challenge that awaits each of us;
our lives are in constant motion.
We must face each challenge
　　with an open heart;
we must also realize that no two
　　lives are the same,
and that each of us has our
　　own unique abilities
to undertake whatever comes
　　our way.

When changes happen in our lives,
what really matters is that we
　　try our best to deal
with the situation.
If we make an effort toward
　　working things out,
then we give ourselves the opportunity
to decide our fate
and make choices about which way
　　our futures may lead us.

Being happy and content doesn't mean
    living in a world of perfect harmony;
rather, it means that you
    allow yourself to flow with
the music that plays in your life.
Enjoy the different melodies
    of each unique day.
Be flexible and easygoing;
you'll be surprised at how much
    better you feel
when you don't try to control everything.
But also be ready to make choices
    and follow through on them,
because they are the decisions
that will influence all aspects
    of your life.
Always remember that positive thinking
    allows the songs in your heart
to make beautiful sounds for everyone
    to enjoy.

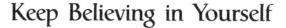

Keep Believing in Yourself

There may be days
when you get up in the morning
and things aren't the way
you had hoped they would be.
That's when you have to
tell yourself that things will get better.
There are times when people
disappoint you and let you down,
but those are the times
when you must remind yourself
to trust your own judgments
and opinions,
to keep your life focused on
believing in yourself
and all that you are capable of.

There will be challenges to face
and changes to make in your life,
and it is up to you to accept them.
Constantly keep yourself headed
in the right direction for you.

It may not be easy at times,
but in those times of struggle
you will find a stronger sense
    of who you are,
and you will also see yourself
developing into the person
you have always wanted to be.

Life is a journey through time,
filled with many choices;
each of us will experience life
in our own special way.
So when the days come
that are filled with frustration
and unexpected responsibilities,
remember to believe in yourself
and all you want your life to be,
because the challenges and changes
will only help you to find
the dreams that you know
are meant to come true for you.